Balancing productivity with wellbeing:

Nurturing success and happiness

James Dewitt

Table of Content

Chapter 1

Understanding the relationship between productivity and wellbeing

Performance will soar when you put people first and then surround them with systems and practices that value their contributions.

With time, the concept of employee well-being has changed. workers' emotional and mental health have taken on a position of significance of their own, and businesses must now pay particular attention to them. businesses are no longer solely worried about the physical well-being of their workers.

It seems to reason that improving an employee's well-being would probably result in favorable developments.

This might include improved performance at work and increased presenteeism, as well as a reduction in health risk as measured by physical, mental, and emotional well-being. Another important element in achieving improved employee well-being is workplace assistance.

What does "employee well-being" mean, and why is it significant?

In the past, physical safety—averting accidents and minimizing injury in the workplace—was associated with employee welfare. But the concept has changed. Employers are now paying more attention to their workers' mental and emotional health.

We all know that stressed-out or exhausted individuals don't function as effectively. Research also supports it. Creating processes and cultures at work that assist workers is fundamental to well-being. It involves paying attention to their issues, both at work and outside of it, and effectively reacting to them. Well-being is impacted by workload. Mental illness does too. It makes sure that line managers can address issues with employees as they emerge and before they get out of hand.

Some company owners may scoff at this. However, increased workplace happiness might lessen instances of presenteeism and absenteeism, which together cost the UK economy £73 billion annually. Better employee productivity and happiness are positively correlated with better workplace wellness levels. Additionally, it often increases a business's efficiency and profitability.

How Does Productivity Work?

Each firm will have a distinct definition of productivity. In the end, it serves as a gauge for worker output. Simply defined, productive workers are more successful and efficient at their jobs, while unproductive workers make fewer positive contributions to a company's success.

When we're not feeling well or when we're preoccupied with domestic issues, concentration, and attention are lost. We do our duties as required. We show up, but it's difficult to come up with original answers and it's simpler to make errors. In these situations, employees always perform below expectations, which lowers corporate productivity.

There are various causes of presenteeism.

1) Excessive workloads may make taking time off challenging

2) A company does not provide paid sick days

3) Fewer workers are taking yearly leave

4) A shortage of personnel to fill in for absent employees.

5) Employees may fear reprimand or punishment for calling in sick.

6) Sucking it up mentality is common in toxic working contexts, which may make disclosing sickness seem weak.

7) Employees can be ashamed to disclose that their mental or physical health is suffering.

Building better workplaces, where workers are assets rather than merely payroll figures, may boost productivity and, therefore, profit.

What's the Relationship Between Productivity and Wellness?

A similar result was reached by a Gallup survey, but this study also drew a link between engaged workers, greater levels of productivity, and higher business profitability. "Organizations that are the best at engaging their employees to achieve earnings-per-share growth that is more than four times that of their competitors."

Similar findings are reached in an article for Forbes magazine: better productivity and reduced staff turnover are both correlated with employee happiness. It also concurs that more firm profitability is correlated with greater employee well-being.

The poll Gallup conducted on its client database also provides some intriguing insight into the relationship between happiness and productivity. It was shown that flexible, engaged workers put in longer hours than the typical worker while yet reporting better levels of well-being. Findings showed that when workers feel inspired, motivated, and encouraged at work, they put in more effort without suffering the same health consequences as those who don't.

- Discrimination
- An overwhelming task
- Poor management communication
- Absence of managerial backing
- And irrational time constraints

The good news is that none of the top 5 Gallup issues can't be resolved by a corporation on its own. A strong HR and management staff is fully capable of handling internal issues. Take solace in the knowledge that you can fix this if employee underperformance is causing your company to struggle.

Unfortunately, one of the largest challenges might sometimes be management. According to a Deloitte survey, 24% of line managers do not think that controlling the workloads of the employees they are responsible for is part of their job description.

Given how closely workload and burnout are now related, this is problematic. It also emphasizes that adding a meditation pod to an office is not enough to promote workplace health. Hot yoga over lunch or beanbags in the boardroom won't help if poor task management is the root of your company's low productivity.

Employees are entitled to care from their employers. This entails helping them before they reach their breaking point and taking a three-month leave of absence.

Therefore, it is crucial to comprehend how wellness and productivity are related.

How to Strengthen the Connection Between Productivity and Well-Being

Ask your staff, who are the closest to the situation. Find out whether they feel supported and comfortable in their position. Ascertain their level of satisfaction with both their own and other people's work. How content are they? Ask them to point out any points of contention or friction in their current position. This could be concerning a particular management or policy.

The Department of Work and Pensions ordered one of the online questionnaire templates for use in the workplace. We also have a piece on our website that examines how companies may assess employee well-being.

A fantastic place to start is by obtaining an accurate image of the corporate culture. Problems may be remedied more quickly (and more easily) if they are discovered early enough. Employees should be encouraged to share their experiences in surveys even if they should remain anonymous.

The topic of well-being should not be brought up just once, but rather daily. If you're unsure of which data to collect and which to disregard, you may always outsource this data collection to an outside organization.

Do surveys or chats with workers reveal any recurring themes? Is there more personnel turnover in one area than others? A decrease in productivity or poor morale might have only one underlying reason. If the problem is workload-related, setting up meditation sessions is of little use. An issue with a line manager won't be resolved by a staff outing.

This is where hiring outside firms to conduct a survey might be useful. Having the data is one thing; understanding how to use the results is quite another.

Employee motivation may be significantly impacted by placing the proper individuals in management positions. Not everyone who is promoted to higher positions has the disposition, expertise, or experience necessary to succeed as a manager or leader. Divisions between management and staff are a result of poor management. They also enable things to go worse.

Those with little firsthand experience will benefit from training. Instead of creating a workplace where workers feel uncomfortable talking about their jobs with others, this does not imply breeding a department of mommy-coddlers. Ideally, there will be enough so that any issues may be identified before they become uncontrollable.

Employees should also get assistance in addition to merely being compensated for the job they accomplish. It is possible to prevent unfair assignment of additional work to workers by routinely assessing workloads and caseloads.

Existing prospects for devoted personnel to progress within the company? Is there a track for promotions? How long do workers normally remain with the company?
 It may be beneficial to make it simpler for workers to switch across departments.

Encouragement for them to enroll in training programs or take on new responsibilities may make them feel more satisfied and often boost their commitment to a firm. Additionally helpful is hiring internally from a trusted pool of talented candidates.

Some businesses provide access to outside counseling services for their employees. This might be a private phone number or perhaps a suggestion to meet with an appropriate therapist. Choosing wellness officers may also be helpful. These are managers or staff that not only provide a point of contact for staff with work-related issues but also serve as guideposts to supporting services.

Be sensible about the workplace of today. In certain firms, flexible working is quite effective. It may draw in fresh talent that might otherwise be inappropriate for a standard 9 to 5 schedule. What does it matter if someone begins work two hours earlier to end two hours sooner as long as the task is done effectively and to the required standard?

Additionally, flexible job arrangements make life simpler for parents. By making appointments simpler to attend, it also encourages workers to meet their wellness requirements. Employers noted fewer sick days during the epidemic when employees worked from home. Additionally, it prevented interactions between healthy and ill employees. Employees save time and money by not having to make a lengthy trip. While simultaneously demonstrating trust, flexibility is allowed.

Employees who feel appreciated and trusted enough to take advantage of customized working conditions will be more productive. Businesses will also become more appealing to potential workers when hiring new staff.

Encourage staff to leave their workstations for breaks. It may be helpful to set up a welcoming kitchen and communal dining area. People might be motivated to get up and away from their screens by negotiating discounts with nearby cafés or meal delivery services.

Breaks provide the body and brain with an opportunity to reset and refocus. It might be beneficial to get some distance from our immediate surroundings and spend some time alone. People like to converse during lunch breaks, which might encourage coworkers to be more honest with one another.

In addition to enhancing physical and mental health, exercise also increases productivity. People who spend too much time at a desk may become lethargic and uninspired. Two more factors lower productivity. A fantastic way to reduce stress is to exercise. Businesses are increasingly deciding to include indoor bikes in their work environments.

Some firms host walking groups around lunchtime, bring yoga instructors for a lesson, or provide discounted gym memberships. People may exercise more while they are working if you set up friendly contests or step or mile goals.

The wellness of employees may be greatly improved by creating a pleasant work environment. Ideal lighting is daylight. The finest workspaces are friendly and bright, where people love working. Employers may provide locations for people to sit down and converse.

A more united team may be created by planning social activities like ordering takeout for lunch and eating it all together. When the weather is nice, outdoor sitting spaces may be fantastic for encouraging individuals to take a break from their workstations.

Programs for employee perks are a good incentive for employees. Employees have access to a variety of special offers and discounts, including discounted gym membership, food delivery services, and even utility bill savings, after employers pay a fee to an outside organization.

Employees may feel more positively engaged with the reasons that matter if their employer partners with a charity or social cause that is well-liked by the workforce and then hosts events or organizes fundraising efforts.

Organizing staff get-togethers and days or evenings out may promote the development of new friendships. With coworkers they connect with rather than supervisors, workers may be more prone to communicate and decompress.

Not only large corporations with limitless vacation time and hot yoga pods prioritize employee welfare. Improved management and staff communication is often the key. It involves having team members who understand the connection between workload and burnout and who can contribute to fostering an honest and open work environment.

It involves identifying when someone is having problems or performing below expectations and helping them get back on track to being not just a productive employee but also a healthier and happier person overall. Employees are a resource. Businesses that put out the effort to maintain a contented and productive staff often discover that the results are an improved and more lucrative operation.

Chapter 2

Exploring the dimensions of wellbeing

The quest for well-being involves finding balance and ongoing progress throughout its absolute aspects. In the minds of many, "wellness" exclusively refers to physical health. The phrase makes people think about blood pressure, exercise, diet, and other topics. But wellness goes well beyond physical health.

The combination of one's physical, mental, and social well-being is known as wellness. The factors that influence the quality of life are intricately intertwined.

Generally speaking, there are various aspects to wellness. Each aspect influences and overlaps the others, and each adds to our feeling of well-being or quality of life. While one dimension may sometimes take center stage over others, neglecting anyone for an extended period has negative implications on general health.

Today, we'll go into detail about 5 dimensions.

Balance is key to living.

No one indicator can assess your general health. Our well-being is influenced by a variety of factors, including the meals we consume and the social circles we maintain.

The symbiotic relationship between the many aspects of well-being will become clearer as you learn more about them. You'll begin to see how everything is related. Your entire health is completed by the relationships between all the components of your wellness.

1. Physical Well-Being

Physical well-being is the easiest aspect of well-being to measure. On a treadmill, you can track calories burnt, hours of sleep, and grams of protein with accuracy. We can observe these figures and comprehend how they impact our bodily well-being.

To assess your physical health, you must take a step back and look at yourself in the mirror. Have you gained or lost any weight recently? Do you feel worn out or drowsy? What color is your skin?

Heart disease, cancer, respiratory conditions, stroke, and accidents are the top killers in the US. These fatalities can be avoided in about half of cases by:

Improving your physical wellness by changing your diet, getting more exercise, and abstaining from risky behaviors.

- Healthy eating

Dietary modifications often include eating more vegetables, consuming less salt, avoiding sugary beverages, and consuming less simple carbohydrates. Keep in mind that this does not entail that you must adopt the strictest super diet or that you may never again drink soda. Instead, focus on implementing smaller, more manageable, and long-lasting dietary modifications. Consider including veggies in a recipe you already like. Every day, swap out one unhealthy beverage for water or tea.

- Physical exercise

Sedentary habits are fatal. People who don't exercise enough are more likely to acquire weight and have other health issues. A sedentary lifestyle might increase your risk of heart disease even if you are not overweight.

Everyone's definition of an active lifestyle is unique. Make careful you just commit to what your body is capable of. Instead of attempting to plan gym time, incorporating exercise into your everyday life often boosts your chances of remaining motivated and getting consistent results. It's fantastic if "getting active" entails frequenting the gym every day. You may get just as much exercise if you take your dog to the park or go gardening. Making a conscious effort to be as active as you can is the key objective.

- Abstain from drugs and hazardous conduct

We can't provide complete protection. Life doesn't come with any assurances. But you may lessen your chances by abstaining from risky habits like smoking (or being around others who smoke), binge drinking, and careless actions like driving recklessly.

2. "Emotional Health"

When compared to physical fitness, emotional wellness has traditionally received less attention, although being just as important. Some individuals are quick to dismiss emotional health as illusory since the results of inadequate psychological care are not always immediately obvious.

However, our lives are significantly impacted by our mental health. For instance, having poor emotional overall health may make us more prone to physical issues.

Your mental mood, your physical health, and your immediate environment are all closely related. Maintaining mental well-being requires attention to your surroundings, food, and social life.
Be careful not to fall into the trap of believing that emotional health can be summed up as either having a psychiatric condition or being "normal."

We should all be careful about how we handle our emotions. Emotional care should not just be a significant issue for individuals who have diagnosable disorders, just as proper eating is not simply a worry for the obese.

Although emotions might be challenging to manage, your emotional well-being is still something you can control. You may become better at managing your emotions by engaging in mental exercises like meditation and practicing positivism. It's not always about suppressing or avoiding unpleasant feelings. You must learn to control your negative emotions and understand how and why they influence you.

Here are some pointers for you.
- Even when difficulties emerge, try to retain a good attitude.
- Find your stress reliever. Time management is important since it reduces stress.
- Find a confidant with whom you may openly discuss your emotions.

- Want to chat? Visit your peer or close buddy.
- Ask for expert assistance when you need it.
- Even when you don't feel like smiling, try it.

3. Social Wellness

Social wellness is the quality of your interpersonal connections. Social connections might include your family, friends, neighbors, and anybody else you stay in touch with.

Because our friends and family help keep us grounded when things are tough, social welfare is crucial. If you need assistance, talk to a trusted friend or relative. Sometimes the knowledge that you have a network of support to fall back on may reduce ongoing stress and give you the courage to take chances and dangers you would otherwise avoid, like relocating or beginning a new career.

Similar to how having bad relationships may harm other aspects of your health. Relationship stress is linked to a variety of mental and physical health problems, according to clinical studies. It's a good idea to pause and consider how your connections are influencing you.

Everyone's definition of wellness will vary. It's alright if you're not a people person. Your connections, not the number of friends you have, are what determine how socially well you are. One strong friendship may sometimes be more effective than a dozen poor ones.

Here are some pointers:

- Get active. There are several clubs, so you're sure to discover one that appeals to you.
- Identify your closest buddies.

- Recognize whether a relationship is unhealthy and cut off if necessary.
- Maintain a healthy balance between your personal and professional obligations.

4. Intellectual Well-Being

Do you challenge your mind? This is one great question you should ask yourself. Your master's degree completion status or IQ score has no bearing on how mentally healthy you are. Our minds are similar to our muscles. To maintain things in good condition, we must utilize them.

We refer to this as "cognitive training," and studies have shown that regular "brain training" may enhance mental abilities including motor coordination and focus. There isn't a lot of information to assist identify which games or hobbies provide the most advantages.

The lesson here is that giving your brain challenges to solve or chances to consider complex issues may be enjoyable.

There are tangential advantages to intellectual well-being. Say, for instance, that you carve out 10 minutes each day from your hectic schedule to do a sudoku problem or play a word game. You are not only using your intellect, but you are also giving your body a break from the demands of work, responsibilities, and daily life.

Here are some pointers:

- Keep up with current events.
- Consider your task seriously and invest some time in research
- If you need assistance, ask your coworker.
- Embrace lifelong learning.

5. Workplace Wellness

Jobs may cause a lot of stress and suffering. Our occupational well-being suffers when we are overworked or unappreciated at work. There is more to your work than a salary. The task you put your effort into should be enjoyable and fulfilling.

You ought to feel assured and successful in what you do. The ability to resolve disagreements and difficulties healthily is what good occupational wellness entails rather than conflicts or problems never occurring.

Not everyone has the option to get up and leave their career in search of one that is more fulfilling. Many individuals are forced to work in mundane occupations since their ideal careers are still out of reach. Be grateful for the chance to pursue the vocation you most want if you have the financial means to do so.

Try to discover methods to combine aspects of your ideal work into the one you now have if you feel like you will never be able to get it. What is it about your ideal job that appeals to you?

To discuss your options with your existing supervisor, try to pinpoint tasks or responsibilities that you find appealing. There could be a method to change your current situation such that it more closely matches your requirements.

Although you have little influence over your colleagues or superiors, maintaining excellent mental health may help you deal with difficult circumstances more effectively. Never let fear of going to work stop you.

Other aspects of your life will begin to suffer if your work is terrible. According to Harvard Medical School, there are clear connections between major depressive illness and generalized anxiety disorder, and workplace stress.

Here are some pointers:

- Preparing for and engaging in work that brings you personal fulfillment and enriches your life in a manner that is compatible with your beliefs, aspirations, and way of life.
- Use your special abilities to do something personally fulfilling and meaningful.

Note.

Your life doesn't suddenly alter. The path to greater well-being and self-care is a slower, more steady one. Before you can alter your life, you first need to change your behaviors.

Set yourself up for success by figuring out which self-improvement techniques are most likely to be effective for you. You may not get the consistent, desirable effects that you're probably looking for by just copying and pasting someone else's health regimen into your own life. Your approach to holistic well-being should be as distinctive as you are because you are.

On average, it takes almost two months for a new habit to truly take hold. For many individuals, developing a good habit is harder than kicking a bad one. To help a new, healthy behavior become a habit, it can be necessary to use a variety of techniques.

Enjoy matching activities with like-minded people, set up incentive systems, spend money on supplements, and start using systematic scheduling. Don't expect the "new you" to emerge in a week, just as the "current you" wasn't created overnight.

Set modest objectives at first.

Smaller adjustments are often easier to handle. Don't undervalue a change because of its magnitude. Usually, the healthier adjustments we make that are more modest have the most long-term effects. Additionally, little alterations are more enduring. If it means you can stick with it for longer than a month, then weekly yoga sessions will benefit you considerably more than daily ones.

So go out and begin to develop yourself. You'll discover that every little adjustment makes the subsequent modification simpler. Try not to attempt it all at once. Give each aspect of well-being the consideration and time it requires. You will feel grateful for your efforts in your mind, body, and spirit.

Chapter 3

Setting priorities and goals

Determining the most important goals for productivity and well-being

The productivity and performance of a business are intimately correlated with the health and happiness of its employees.

The U.S. Surgeon General published a new Framework for Health and Workplace Wellbeing in October 2022 that critically emphasizes five fundamental ideas that promote physically and psychologically fit employees.

Some individuals believe that more production equates to decreased well-being. Those folks are mistaken. They could fall prey to management systems that do not comprehend the essence of intellectual work. Note:

- Your well-being directly impacts your productivity;
- When you're productive, your well-being tends to improve—but only to a point.
- You are meeting your obligations to both yourself and your employer by taking care of yourself.

These actions given below will help you become more productive.

1. Setting clear priorities is the first step. Make a fast classification of the most crucial aspects of your life at the moment. Here's my own:

Health first, then loved ones and close friends then work

Please consider why this is so and what it could indicate for the future if your health and intimate connections are not at their best.

We can begin the process now that we have reached agreement on your goals.

- Personal hygiene

A French term called "life hygiene" roughly translates to "lifestyle" in English.

In such cases, we are expressing the obvious, yet the obvious frequently has to be spoken.

Physical activity
This is a must.

It will improve your attitude and concentration in addition to benefiting your health.

- Sleep

Your brain learns information in this way. Make improving your sleep routine a top priority if you don't already have one.

- Posture

So when sitting, you should have a good posture, right? Yes, but not enough for the majority of people. Even so, you'll probably have excruciating back aches.

One's life may be changed by a standing desk. It won't be sufficient either, therefore you'll need a solution that allows you to alternate between sitting and standing for two reasons:

When you initially start, standing all day might be challenging.
As many problems may arise from standing all day as from sitting.

Take frequent pauses and get moving before starting anything. As much as you can, switch up your positions.

Finally, if all of this is still insufficient (and I predict it won't be for many of you), study yoga. The most effective method for treating back pain is daily deep yoga muscle relaxation.

Bonus: A crash course in yoga
Lay on your back on the ground. Breathe in for 5 to 7 seconds, hold for 2, and then exhale for 9 seconds. As much as you can, try to relax your body. daily for 10 minutes. You're doing yoga, which is wonderful.

2. Food
Do not undervalue how much the food you are consuming may make you feel miserable.

I was a food scientist some years ago. Years of study on what you should probably eat may be summed up in the following haiku:

- Mostly veggies, but a little bit of everything.
- Vegetables, indeed.
- Keeping your circadian rhythm healthy
- Most insomniacs just have an improper circadian rhythm, sometimes known as an "internal clock". Pay attention to it.

The most crucial piece of advice I can give you is to spend roughly 10 minutes outdoors in the morning. Your internal clock will be set to "morning" when morning light enters your eyes.

I suggest listening to the complete Huberman Podcast for further advice on this subject and as a wonderful source for scientifically informed tools for your well-being in general.

3. Focusing noise-canceling headphones

If the noises around you or the absence of music are making it difficult for you to concentrate, they will be a huge assistance. If you work in an open environment, it could even be required.

Select a style that won't cause you any discomfort when you wear it for lengthy periods (you don't want to work hard to prevent back problems just to experience head pains). If you have the money, Sony's WH-1000 XM4 is a good option.

- Isolate yourself. OR, don't.

Some individuals do best in a room by themselves. Some individuals do better in the presence of others. Try and see what works for you if you have the means to do so.

- Using the Pomodoro method

On that subject, there are several manuals, therefore I won't go into them all. The general idea is to work in 50-minute cycles interspersed with 10-minute breaks.

You should practice Deep work throughout those 50 minutes of work. Avoid any distractions and practice maintaining attention.

I strongly advise you to stretch throughout the ten-minute pauses.

When I say that the Pomodoro method is the most crucial productivity tool for remote work, I'm not joking.

Even though the Pomodoro approach works well for certain individuals, a lot of them don't use it in the end. A classic issue is knowing something works but not implementing it. Don't be this person; if something works for you, stick with it.

Note that the inverse is also true. If something doesn't work for you, alter it immediately rather than sticking with it.

- Stimulants

As long as coffee is used moderately and doesn't interfere with your sleep, it works excellent as a stimulant.

- Two or more large screens

Many businesses looked for ways to increase staff productivity. The only two things they discovered to be effective were coffee and larger displays.

Consider purchasing at least one larger screen if you operate on a tiny laptop screen.

4. Create a Room

Cleaning your surroundings: A clean environment leads to a clean mind.

Your surroundings will also be chaotic if your brain is chaotic. When your surroundings are chaotic, so is your mind.

This holds for both your physical surroundings and your virtual environment: all of the data on your computer are adding to your mental workload. Make sure to tidy up all of your areas, including your desktop and the one inside of your computer.

- Clear your mind

If you can't control your tension, you can't control your thoughts.

Regularly practicing meditation can help you concentrate more effectively by immediately honing your concentration abilities and will also rid your brain of unneeded clutter.

- Enhancing the code

Technical debt is not only terrible for your well-being but also your productivity. This page explains why in more detail. Therefore, reduce your technological debt. Make it as compact as you can

The Marie Kondo technique is a terrific way to organize your physical, emotional, and digital spaces.

5. Work methods
Although being able to concentrate is beneficial, it won't help you much if your workflow is poor.

The religion of TDD is test-driven development. And I'm involved. This approach is one we continue to promote since it is effective.

TDD is quite hard to master; similar to the game of Go, even if you are familiar with the rules, you may still perform poorly. To genuinely perform successfully, years and years of practice are required.

Even if you are terrible at TDD, it still saves you time in the long and intermediate term. Short-term time savings are another benefit of TDD proficiency.

- AI is your ally.

Although we are unlikely to be replaced by artificial intelligence anytime soon, employing AI will unquestionably increase your productivity by orders of magnitude. I'm not sponsored by Github, but I'll say it anyhow: Copilot is more than worth the $10 monthly fee.

And if you don't know anything, don't hesitate to ask ChatGPT as soon as possible. The new Google is AI.

While ChatGPT did not write this book, it did write the majority of my automated tests for work. Simply copy-paste your class, request some tests, and you're 80% there.

6. Don't Go Overboard

The drawback of improved productivity is that it will allow you to put in more hours.

Working a lot has the drawback that you could work too much.

Working too much can hinder your productivity since you'll get unwell as a result.

Remarkably more intense than non-deep labor, deep work is just that—deep work. You probably won't be able to write 8 hours of your finest code every day without quickly becoming exhausted.

Maintain self-control and self-respect; this is a marathon, not a sprint.

Conclusion
You'll be substantially happier and more productive if you put what we spoke about here into practice. I vouch for my statement.

Chapter 4

Time management for a balanced life

Work-life balance, as the name would imply, entails striking a balance between your professional and personal lives. Even though many individuals may understand how important work-life balance is, relatively few people manage to do so.

In my book "**how to boost productivity** ", I extensively highlighted the concept of time management. You should explore the resources contained in that guide. It will be of great help to you. However, in this chapter, there is sufficient information to guide you through efficient time use.

How is a work-life balance achieved?

Time management is important. The work-life balance you maintain each day will depend on how you spend the time you have available. Utilize time management strategies that will help you recognize what is most important to you, and put these strategies into daily practice.

Unfortunately, a lot of individuals are caught in a vicious loop where their personal life are prioritized above their careers. Find a time-management strategy that works for you as well. Establish objectives and change your surroundings to cut down on distractions. Take action, and when you need to, take a break.

According to data, just 66% of American professionals successfully combine their work and personal lives. When you consider that 88% of employees report feeling stressed out at work, it is obvious that finding a work-life balance is essential to leading a less stressful and higher-quality life.

Why then do so many individuals struggle with work-life balance? One valid explanation might be that many people are just unaware of the significance of work-life balance. They may not be aware of the risks a poor work-life balance poses to their physical and psychological health.

The effects of not having a work-life balance

The effects of a poor work-life balance will differ from person to person. However, increasing stress is virtually always a factor in all ways. Your body and mind may suffer when you don't maintain that balance between your job and personal life.

Think about the repercussions on your body. Lack of work-life balance may make you perpetually exhausted and leave you with little to no energy to concentrate on your priorities. Your body may become stiff, resulting in muscular spasms and discomfort.

Lack of a work-life balance has a lot of emotional repercussions as well. Lack of enough sleep may raise stress, which increases your risk of developing depression and anxiety. The combined mental and physical effects may cause twice as much injury, leaving you exhausted.

Time management tips for balancing work and life

You can attain a work-life balance with the aid of time management. It's crucial since your time management skills will decide whether you succeed in striking that balance or not. In other words, work-life balance is simpler to attain when you are deliberate with your time.

Given this information, using time management skills is the best approach to begin achieving a work-life balance. The appropriate methods will not only enable you to see where your time is being spent daily, but they will also enable you to free up more time so that you may concentrate on the things that are most important to you.

1. Decide what you are responsible for. Establishing your daily workload is the first step in attaining work-life balance. You may determine if you're taking on too many obligations and where most of your day is going by understanding the professional and personal chores for which you are accountable.

Start by forming two columns by drawing a line along the center of a sheet of paper. Responsibilities for the workplace will be included in the first column, and those for personal matters will be listed in the second.

Next, make a list of all the everyday tasks you are responsible for at work. The personal duties column should be treated similarly.

You'll be able to summarize your day after you've done this. Are you juggling too many obligations? Are there any obligations you can discharge? If so, consider your options for assigning the duty to another person or eliminating it. The goal is to limit your to-do list to essential daily tasks.

2. Choose your priorities.
Your priorities may be listed after your obligations have been listed. Here is where you pause to consider what is most important to you. Your priorities may be both personal and professional. Understanding what you want to accomplish with your time is the aim of this phase.

Compare the results of the previous phase to your priorities using the responses. Do your obligations match the things that are most important to you? What choices do you have to fix this problem if they don't? What can you do to give your priorities more time?

 As you proceed through the next action, keep these questions in mind.

   3. Set both personal and professional objectives.
Do the same for your personal and professional objectives as you did for the division and listing of your obligations. Consider everything you wish to accomplish as well as your ultimate aim. The purpose of this stage is to get you ready to start managing your time more effectively by identifying how you would want to utilize it.

Divide your objectives into personal and professional categories in the same way that you did with your list of obligations.

The secret to striking a balance between work and life is to be aware of how you spend your time and to translate this awareness into an action plan that is focused on your objectives.

4. Plan ahead

All of your preparation will come together in this phase. You can use this knowledge to create a sound strategy that will serve as your daily guide now that you are completely aware of what you need to do, what you want to accomplish, and where you want to go.

Start by visualizing your day as a clean slate devoid of any obligations or duties. A blank timetable that divides the day into hours, beginning when you get up and ending when you go to bed, may be made.

Then, include the things you need to do in your calendar. Ensure that your professional objectives and your everyday obligations are in line.

How much time remains after accounting for your obligations? Utilize that time and think about your objectives and aspirations. If necessary, rank them in order of significance. Add the most crucial activities that correspond to your objectives and priorities to complete your daily plan.

Make every effort to plan your days so that work, relaxation, and personal leisure are all given equal weight.

5. Determine your method.
If you discover that planning out your day isn't quite enough to fulfill your demands for time management, consider looking for a method that suits you. Several time-management strategies may assist you in achieving work-life harmony. Several of these methods include:

- Using a Pomodoro
- The matrix of Important and Urgent
- Using the Pareto principle

- The GTD method (Getting Things Done).

Test them out to see which suits your requirements best. Implementing these strategies should be considerably simpler for you since you already know what your obligations, priorities, and objectives are.

If you discover a method that works, continue with it and take note of the advantages it offers you as you get closer to your goal of work-life balance.

6. Change your surroundings

Your surroundings have a significant impact on your productivity and, therefore, on how well you manage your time. You can find yourself taking longer than required to finish your duties if your surroundings are filled with distracting items or instruments. As a result, finding a balance between work and life is challenging.

Make sure any obstructive and harmful objects are distant from you when you sit down to finish your duties and chores to address this issue. Your mobile phone, for example, can distract you and make you waste time.

By eliminating distractions, you may make sure that your work hours are only for work. This will increase your productivity at work and provide you with more time for the things that are important to you.

7. Do something

The ideal strategy to use when dealing with a problem with work-life balance is a solution-oriented one. There won't be much you can do to remedy your issue if you realize it but don't do something about it. Your work-life balance problem will develop as a result of you wasting essential time.

Make an effort to always be learning and to respond when an issue emerges. This may include attending a time management class, picking up a new skill, or just speaking with a trusted friend or family member about your work-life balance concerns.

The goal is to maintain a problem-solving mindset that enables you to recognize and respond to issues as they emerge.

8. Rest

One of the most crucial components of establishing work-life balance is probably this. It is crucial to get enough sleep since it is the way to strike a balance between your personal and professional lives.

The strategy of "rest when you can" just does not work to accomplish this aim. Rest must be given top importance.

Always be aware of your bodily and mental well-being if you want to assist yourself with rest more often. Listening to your body and mind when they express obvious signals of weariness can help you prevent burnout in the future. As burning yourself out wastes more time than just taking a break when you need it, resting is crucial to time management.

Conclusion

Time management is essential for attaining a work-life balance. The amount of balance you keep each day will depend on how you spend the time you have. Unfortunately, a lot of individuals are caught in a vicious loop where their personal life are prioritized above their careers.

The best method to deal with this major issue is to use time management strategies that help you recognize what is most important to you and organize your time following these principles. You may do that by using the time management strategies we've discussed here.

Chapter 5

Embracing mindfulness and self-care

Stress is a part of life. However, persistent stress may have negative effects on our physical health, feelings of wellbeing, and general quality of life. While people are predisposed to be able to handle some stress and even to weather brief times of severity, this is not always the case.

And the effects on our physical and emotional health may be severe when stressful experiences are multiplied—when issues, concerns, and sadness build up. Anxiety, depression, sleeplessness, high blood pressure, and heart disease are just a few of the devastating effects that chronic stress may have on our lives. Even our immunity may be compromised.

Regrettably, difficult life situations seldom come with much notice.

Every one of us will eventually be pushed to our limits, even if our life is generally in balance and we feel capable of handling adversity when it arises. We'll experience overload. We'll have a hard time managing our emotions, our workload, and life in general.

To succeed in life, it is crucial to understand how to handle stress. And doing so via mindfulness training not only enables you to manage stressful situations more skillfully and without difficulty, but it also gives you useful life skills, such as:

- Increased self-awareness helps us to better grasp what we need at any given time, especially when we start to feel overwhelmed.

- increased ability for forgiveness and compassion for both ourselves and others.
- more resiliency, which makes it simpler to go over difficulties.
- improved capacity for maintaining equilibrium and stability under pressure.
- having a higher feeling of acceptance and ease generally, as well as being more aware of being present at the moment.

The issue of stress management is popular for good reason. Everybody goes through stressful times in both their personal and professional life. Being under stress is a natural element of being human.

A clinical partner of the University of Massachusetts Medical School, the University of Massachusetts Memorial Health Care, states that "The detrimental consequences of chronic stress and their influence on the quality of our lives is well established. When left unchecked, our bodily reactions to stress may result in bad health, yet they often go unrecognized until symptoms or circumstances make them obvious.

What is the process of mindfulness?

You are invited by mindfulness to concentrate on being acutely aware of what you are experiencing and feeling right now, without interpretation or judgment.

Who or what is mindful?
The definition of mindfulness according to Mindfulness.org is "the fundamental human capacity to be fully present, aware of where we are and what we are doing, and not overly reactive or overwhelmed by what is going on around us."

Mindfulness aims to encourage attention to our sometimes underappreciated mental, bodily, and emotional realities. It arouses our innate curiosity, allowing us to be fully present in every situation without passing judgment. Self-awareness, self-compassion, and knowledge are all energized.

How can mindfulness improve focus while reducing stress?

Our minds often stray and rapidly get enmeshed in familiar ideas and pondering feelings. With effort, we may develop the self-awareness required to identify unprocessed ideas and emotions and stop them from controlling our higher, more rational thinking. We can then more simply and regularly use our problem-solving, creativity, and executive functioning skills.

The prefrontal cortex (PFC), the brain region that serves as the "boss" or manager of our thoughts and emotions, is strengthened by mindfulness training. The PFC controls our ability to organize, make goals, think flexibly, learn, and reason. It also has an impact on how we interact with others.

Focus, performance, and interpersonal relationships are all enhanced as a result of mindfulness. Mindfulness also helps to alleviate mental, emotional, and physical stress. Living in the present now by making use of our five senses (sound, smell, touch, taste, and sight) and our breath gives us the abilities we need to deal with difficult circumstances that come up during the day.

Mindfulness training helps us to be attentive to our thoughts and emotions, notice them, and respond purposefully and with positive intentions rather than automatically responding to them. These advantages of mindfulness may help people manage their stress better and live more peaceful and satisfying lives.

Do I practice mindfulness?

Believing we are unable is a typical obstacle to mindfulness practice. Frequently, we erroneously believe that if our thoughts, feelings, or physical sensations like pain enter our awareness, we are doing something wrong. Being conscious of what is occurring is a necessary component of mindfulness, which indicates that we are doing it appropriately.

Being mindful does not entail clearing our brains, but rather allowing the current moment to occupy our minds. One aspect of the practice is to become aware of our thoughts, emotions, and physical sensations. Our brains learn to live in the present moment by practicing the skills of naming what is occurring, letting go of it, and coming back to our main focus.

Mindfulness benefits

Numerous advantages of mindfulness for reducing stress include improvements to our physical, mental, and cognitive well-being. The following advantages of mindfulness for physical, emotional, and mental health are shown by positive psychology.

What studies on mindfulness reveal

There is a ton of reliable data on the benefits of practicing mindfulness to reduce stress.

1. An increase in working memory.
Research in the American Psychological Association demonstrates a connection between mindfulness and improved functional memory. According to the research, doing enough mindfulness practice may be able to prevent you from losing your ability to function at your best under pressure.

2. A better knowledge of one's mental processes.
A 2014 research that appeared in the Open Journal of Medical Psychology links mindfulness to a reduction in unfavorable thought patterns.

3. Lessening of emotional sensitivity.
There is evidence to support mindfulness's contribution to lowering emotional reactivity and aiding in emotion regulation.

Using mindfulness to decrease stress

Before starting any of the mindfulness activities that follows, practice these tips for slowing your mind.

- Make yourself comfy. This might be doing so while laying down on the floor or while sitting upright in a chair. Avoid laying in bed so that you don't connect mindfulness meditation with sleeping.

- Relax both your body and face. Your whole body and mind may relax even more as a result of doing this since it can aid in the neurological relaxation of your central nervous system.
- Increase the duration gradually after starting with 30 seconds. Your day may be significantly impacted by even a little period of pure awareness.

Guidelines for implementing mindfulness

This is a summary of quick and easy mindfulness activities that you may simply include in your life to reduce stress. They will assist you in beginning a mindfulness practice by applying basic mindfulness methods to common events.

1. Your breathing should be your main focus.

Become conscious of the in and outflow of your breath. As you breathe in and out, pay attention to how your stomach rises and falls. Pay attention to how you're breathing.

2. Eat with awareness.

Establish a relaxing atmosphere for eating. Get rid of all distractions, including your phone and media. Concentrate on the flavor, texture, appearance, and scent of your meal. While chewing, close your eyes and express thankfulness for the nourishment provided by food.

3. Driving.

Turn off any commotion including music and phone alerts. Take hold of the steering wheel. Are your fingers relaxed or clenched? To respond calmly to any changes in speed or stop lights, give yourself plenty of room while you follow traffic. Take a deep breath and focus more on what you are doing than where you are going.

4. A careful stroll.

Take a stroll or exercise as you are able. On your face, feel the wind or the sun. Smell the nearby grass and trees for aromas. Take time to hear the breeze and the birds. Observe the beauty around you. Consider your reaction to this.

5. Mindfulness at work.

Take frequent pauses to relax and get away from your job. If you have privacy, close your eyes and pay attention to your breathing. As you breathe in and out, feel it in your body.

Without making any attempts, just relax into your breath. Think about something for which you are thankful after a short while, and experience the feelings that go along with it. Start working when you've opened your eyes. Take note of the impact that these 1-3 minutes make.

6. Enhance sleep.

Take some quiet time after supper and for at least an hour before bed. Go somewhere quiet and take a deep breath. Focus on your breathing and close your eyes. Take a notepad, write on paper with a pen rather than using technology, and maintain silence.

Allow ideas to come to you, then capture them. Because you are giving your brain time to think, it often happens that the ideas that would have kept you awake at night may come to mind during this period. Put the paper away in a location where you can find it again tomorrow.

7. Anxious emotions.

Recognize when you start to feel down or nervous. What notion are you having? Observe your gut feeling. Think about how accurate the notion is, then swap it out with something uplifting and accurate.

8. Establishing peace.

Bring your attention to your breath if a meeting is stressing you out. Breathe slowly, taking four-second breaths in and eight-second breaths out. This makes it easier for you to feel less stressed and think clearly and behave accordingly.

9. Actively hearing.

Instead of chatting during a discussion, pay attention. Pay attention to the spoken words as well as the accents. Keep an eye out for the person's body language and the way they make you feel.

Without forming an opinion or answer, just be present with their message. While you learn more about the individual and their message, the other person will feel heard.

10.   Use all of your senses.

We may go from being stressed to being at ease by concentrating on our five senses. It is a kind of mindfulness that you may use to refocus and recharge at any time and from anywhere.

Eyes closed, concentrate intently on what you hear. Take a close look at what you hear. This is very relaxing in a natural environment. Now concentrate on what you smell.

Be very aware of your feelings. Grasp your face. Feel the surface's texture as it is in front of you. Consider how a chair or the ground supports your body.

Taste. Try taking a drink of water or just observing what your taste receptors are detecting right now.

Get your eyes open. Keep your attention on something in front of you that is beautiful or significant. Consider how a tree's leaves are changing in the wind, or concentrate carefully on a piece of art.

Be aware and calm.

Chapter 6

Building healthy habits for success

Adopting good habits that increase well-being and productivity

Competing obligations, impossible deadlines, consecutive Zoom sessions, a stuffed inbox, working out, and getting lunch... It could seem hard to enhance your productivity since there is so much to accomplish.

Relax. You may enhance your productivity and feel energized and successful rather than fatigued and overwhelmed by kicking negative habits and forming new ones.

How Do Habits Work?

Habits are daily rituals and routines that we naturally carry out, such as making coffee, walking the dog, or practicing meditation.

We all have many habits. Some habits are engrained, such as tooth brushing and shoe-tying.

Others, such as visiting the gym or taking a daily multivitamin, need effort and attention to become routines. Others are undesirable habits that may hurt well-being and productivity, such as compulsively eating junk food or continually checking email.

We are accustomed beings. According to Duke University research, about 45% of actions tend to be repeated in the same place practically daily. The Power of Habit author Charles Duhigg claims that habits are made up of straightforward cue-routine-reward cycles.

Consider the scenario where you wish to start strength training consistently using resistance bands to boost your metabolism and improve your capacity to lift big items. You leave the bands near the TV remote control rather than putting them in your dresser drawer. You know when to start your routine when the TV is on.

Following your workout, treat yourself to a tasty protein-based beverage to reward yourself and replenish your muscles.

A negative habit is more difficult to break. The greatest approach is to switch a bad habit for a good one rather than exerting willpower, which is quickly depleted and isn't nearly as strong as people assume. For instance, your regular visit to the vending machine when you purchase a candy bar and a beverage is triggered every afternoon when you feel weary and hungry (your signal).

Simply have healthy snacks like almonds, pumpkin seeds, or dry-roasted edamame at your desk to break the habit. You may also get a colorful water bottle and flavoring drops to organically improve the taste of the water without adding extra sugar or calories.

You may establish a new pattern when you feel the urge to eat (your cue) by grabbing your nutritious snack and water bottle and going for a quick walk instead of purchasing a candy bar and drink. You feel more energized and less worried as a result. This simple change helps you control your weight and lose weight over time by reinforcing the new pattern and putting an end to the old.

You now know how habits function. **Here are 8 behaviors you may adopt to become more productive.**

1. Have a nutritious breakfast.
While skipping breakfast and heading straight to work may seem like the most efficient method to accomplish more, having a healthy breakfast can jump-start your metabolism and have a significant, positive

influence on your productivity throughout the day.

A nutritious breakfast gives your brain the energy it needs to concentrate, which utilizes 20–25% of the body's energy in the form of glucose (also known as blood sugar).

A mix of protein, good fats, and complex—rather than refined—carbohydrates makes for the finest breakfast for maintaining your energy levels and productivity. This entails leaving the bagels, muffins, and donuts out. Instead, have a peanut butter and whole wheat sandwich, a breakfast sandwich, or a wrap with eggs, refried beans, and salsa.

Alternately, have hot or overnight oats with chia and flax seeds along with a glass of water flavored with high-protein collagen powder.

2. Use caffeine with caution.

64% of Americans, according to a Gallup survey, consume at least one cup of coffee daily. Studies demonstrate that caffeine, a central nervous system stimulant, may enhance memory and cognitive performance when used in moderation.

The efficiency of brain activity may be increased by consuming coffee and glucose, which are both healthy carbohydrates, according to research from the University of Barcelona. Dopamine, a hormone that makes you feel happy, as well as energy, particularly when you're fatigued, are both increased by caffeine.

It has also been shown to lessen inflammation, which may assist ease discomfort and prevent you from being as productive as you would want to be.

Wait an hour or two until your natural energy levels start to decline before drinking your tea or coffee to optimize the effects of caffeine. Cortisol, your stress hormone, is produced at its peak levels first thing in the morning. Instead of downing a nitro brew to stay focused and increase productivity, take little doses of caffeine throughout the day.

Drink a tiny cup of coffee or go for green tea instead, which has fewer health advantages due to its reduced caffeine content, such as enhancing blood flow and decreasing cholesterol. Additionally, studies have shown that drinking green tea may enhance cognitive performance.

You could also wish to provide guarana, a Brazilian native plant, used to make energy drinks. According to one research, it encouraged employees to focus on their work and finish it more quickly.

However, consuming too much coffee may prevent you from getting a restful night's sleep, cause jitteriness, and heighten anxiety. The safe daily dose for healthy persons is often up to 400 mg.

3. Eat your frog.

Mark Twain is credited for saying, "Eat your frog," adding that it's preferable to carry out this task first thing in the morning if you must do so. Additionally, it's recommended to consume the largest frog first if you have to consume two frogs.

Twain intended that you should start the day's most difficult work first thing in the morning. You'll experience a feeling of success and relief after finishing your most difficult work. This behavior will not only boost productivity but will also help you avoid putting things off.

Make a to-do list at the end of each day or the first thing in the morning to develop the habit of eating your frog. Choose your top three priorities for the day before you start working on them. Put the most difficult and crucial task—your frog—at the top of your list. just carry it out!

4. The right supplements
A decent vitamin and mineral supplement that is appropriate for your age and gender may help increase attention, energy, and productivity while not completely replacing a balanced diet.

Make sure you get enough vitamin D, which is crucial for immunity, bone health, and attention (many individuals are low, particularly in the winter). The B vitamins, particularly folate, niacin, and B-12, all contribute to the creation of energy. Vitamin C, which is necessary for the production of norepinephrine, a neurotransmitter that regulates attention, is also crucial.

Make sure you consume adequate Omega-3 fatty acids to improve brain health and guarantee peak performance. Walnuts, chia seeds, and flaxseeds are other excellent dietary sources, as are fatty seafood like salmon and sardines.

5. Take a break for yourself.
Although you would believe that working constantly boosts productivity, the reality is that most individuals can't concentrate for more than an hour or two. You'll get more done if you take frequent breaks, particularly if you use a computer a lot.

According to research in the journal Ergonomics, taking regular, brief breaks from computer use—of approximately three minutes—increases productivity and well-being.

The ideal approach is to get into the habit of arranging work in brief intervals that are followed by breaks. Try several things to determine what suits you the best. Try working for 25 to 30 minutes and taking a five-minute break, or for 90 minutes and taking a ten to fifteen-minute break.

Taking a whiff of some essential oils is a quick practice to try out during your break that may improve your mood, attention, and productivity. Lemon, rosemary, peppermint, and sweet orange are all recommended for use.

Additionally, create a computer or phone reminder to remind you to get up, stretch, and move around once each hour. Your back will appreciate it, and you'll lower your chances of developing heart disease and putting on weight.

According to research, utilizing a standing desk and switching between standing and sitting may boost your mood, give you more energy, and raise your productivity.

6. Throw out multitasking
You're probably thinking, as I am, that multitasking boosts productivity. That is a total fabrication. According to Stanford

University research, excessive multitasking might impair cognitive control and decrease productivity. It would be like connecting the toaster, microwave, and hair dryer all into the same outlet to write your work presentation while watching the news and preparing dinner.

Not only will you stress yourself out more, but you'll also lose focus and blow a brain fuse. Do one item at a time and take your time. While you're at it, reduce interruptions by putting your mobile phone away and just checking email a few times each day.

Additionally, if you tend to delay or feel overwhelmed, divide big jobs into smaller ones and work on each one individually.

7. Advancing, not perfecting

The devaluation of one's self, the suppression of innovation, and the rejection of novel ideas all harm productivity. Furthermore, perfectionism might hinder your progress by encouraging procrastination.

Get into the habit of producing your best work while admitting your mistakes and concentrating on progress rather than perfection rather than trying to accomplish everything flawlessly. Make a note of all your accomplishments and all you managed to get done for the day at the conclusion. You'll appreciate how industrious you were and feel content.

Ask for assistance if you are having trouble with a job and are making hopeless attempts to finish it. Your strength might be a coworker's weakness, and vice versa.

8. Self-care
One of the finest productivity habits you can adopt is finding a balance between work and leisure and making time for your physical, mental, and spiritual well-being. Get 7-8 hours of sleep each night, exercise often, eat

wholesome meals and snacks, remain hydrated, and participate in things that energize you and help you recharge if you want to be extremely productive.

So, are you willing to start these new routines?
Whether your habits are good or harmful, you must take specific actions to change how you feel about them and improve your overall well-being.

Chapter 7

Finding flow in work and life

How to Achieve Flow and Happiness in Your Work and Personal Life: The Flow State

What is flow state precisely, and why do so many people gush about its advantages?
A corner table at a coffee shop a little distance from my house is one of my favorite spots to write.

I feel more in the correct frame of mind when I combine the aroma of coffee with the noise of the café and sit on the bench seat with one leg beneath me.

The hours just seem to fly by. The alert reminding me that it was time for school pickup had startled me more than once, making me realize how quickly the hours had passed.

This location suits me because of it. It facilitates my ability to flow.

But what is a flow state precisely, and why do so many people like it?

To teach you how to achieve and sustain a flow state for increased productivity and enjoyment, this chapter will discuss the flow state and its elements.

What Is a State of Flow?

Mihály Cskszentmihályi, a psychologist, coined the term "flow state theory" in the 1970s.

Cskszentmihályi researched how individuals may continue to do effectively and for pleasure even when they are not paid externally, together with the co-founder of positive psychology Jeanne Nakamura. Starting with highly successful people, such as doctors and dancers, their research later included a broad range of individuals.

The scientists found that individuals, regardless of class, culture, age, or other factors, find enjoyment in experiencing the most intense moments of being immersed in an activity rather than in leisure or rest.

When one is completely concentrated on a job and output comes readily, an intrinsic motivational condition known as "flow" emerges.

According to a 2016 research report, flow is:

"the psychological mental state of a person who is immersed in an activity with energetic concentration, optimal enjoyment, full involvement, and intrinsic interests, and who is usually focused, motivated, positive, energized, and aligned with the task at hand."

In essence, you are in a flow state of mind when you are so preoccupied with your activity that you entirely forget about everything else, time slows down, and your workflows easily.

In the realm of productivity, this is also known as "getting in the zone" and is quite popular.

You are in a flow state of mind when you are so preoccupied with your activity that you entirely disregard everything else, time slows down, and your workflows without effort.

Structure of a Flow State

Even while we may seem to be "in the zone" or working hard at times, we are not actually in a flow state. Several elements must work together to create flow.

Eight factors, according to Csikszentmihalyi, go together with the sensation of flow:

- Specified objectives that get a rapid response
- a keen concentration on a certain subject
- Challenges and abilities must coexist in harmony.
- a feeling of power
- a sense of comfortability
- a shift in the sense of time
- Bringing awareness and action together
- an inherent trait, drive, or motivation

For a flow state to exist, the first three conditions must be satisfied. The other components, which may or may not be present at the same time, explain how we feel when engaged in an activity in a flow state.

What Characterizes an Optimal Flow State?

An individual has the best experience when they are joyful as a result of bringing order to awareness. He contends that when a previous expectation is realized, surpassed, or a surprising accomplishment is made, we are joyful.

The emphasis on awareness in the psychology of flow is one of my favorite features. It applies a basic principle of everyday living—being totally in the present moment—to work, making it more pleasurable. Being present, concentrating only on one job, and taking pleasure in your work while doing it are all requirements for being in a flow state.

Being present, concentrating only on one job, and taking pleasure in your work while doing it are all requirements for being in a flow state.

Flow State advantages

Beyond just making work more pleasurable, the flow has several advantages. Several benefits are listed below:

1. A rise in originality.

When doing creative work, flow states are often encountered, which promotes a more intense level of artistic and creative inspiration.

2. Improved efficiency.

Research has shown that flow states may improve performance and output in a variety of contexts, such as the arts, learning, and sports.

3. More contentment and happiness.

In a flow state, we are more content with what we are doing, which makes it more pleasurable. A task is more gratifying and satisfying when it is enjoyable.

4. Growth and learning are ever-present.
To maintain flow, which signifies mastery of a skill, we must constantly seek out new challenges and knowledge.

5. Greater degrees of joy.
There is evidence that flow moods are connected to higher levels of contentment and joy. A flow state produces a long-lasting sense of contentment and well-being.

What Underlies the Flow State Scientifically?
What precisely is going on within to produce this mystical condition, then?

Our brains adapt neurobiologically in a manner that promotes mental flexibility.

Our attention narrows when we get into a flow state. The subconscious mind takes the place of our slower, more inefficient conscious thought. Known as transient hypofrontality, this phenomenon. It's a big part of why we feel "flowy."

The mental processes that would prevent us from making hasty judgments are blocked, as well as our higher cognitive capacities. The scene resembles something from a dream.

Additionally, it has been shown using functional magnetic resonance imaging (fMRI) that flow conditions reduce self-monitoring activity in the dorsolateral prefrontal cortex. When we quiet our inner critic and remain judgment-free of ourselves, we become more creative.

In a flow state, you may also locate a lot of molecules that make you feel good, such as endorphins, serotonin, dopamine, and norepinephrine. Particularly attention, pattern identification, and lateral thinking—the "three horsemen of rapid-fire problem-solving," as Time put it—are improved by these in all performance-related domains.

When these three important neurobiological alterations are together, we experience easy, pleasurable, and free-flowing mental activity. That is very cool.

What Does Flow State Look Like in Practice?

You may be saying to yourself, "Wow, that's great! But how exactly does this operate?

We have a wide range of opportunities and methods for entering a flow state. The flow state may be experienced while working, going about daily tasks, or engaging in other pursuits like sports or the arts. Here are some examples of how a flow state could develop.

While working

Writing at Work: Finding Your Flow. Do you recall the tale I told at the start of this article? Writers who like discussing a subject might easily get lost in their ideas and enter a state of flow. I have a hard time keeping track of time while I am writing something I adore!

Artists. Similar to how a painter might find themselves in a flow state as soon as they get into it, time can fly by just like the paint on the canvas for a painter who finds their rhythm.
employees with knowledge.

Anyone who "thinks for a living" on the job may discover that they often experience flow states while working. Workers who are given duties that allow them to focus only on the project may feel the flow.

The Flow's Application to Other Areas of Life

Education. People who "overlearn" things or abilities may enter a state of flow. By setting objectives that are just a little beyond their ability level, students may attain the flow by expanding their thoughts to greater heights.

Sports. Pushing oneself in a manageable but difficult fashion just a little bit over their comfort zones allows athletes to enter flow states. Athletes may feel less self-conscious and more secure in their skills while they are in the zone.

Both prayer and meditation. This one should go without saying. You may achieve a sense of flow when you concentrate your thoughts on your meditation or prayer. Following Headspace, "a mind that is trained to be more present and at ease with itself — calmer, clearer, and content — is more likely to experience the flow state because we are training in non-distraction and focus."
musician in a flow mood while mixing

What Techniques Can Be Used To Enter a Flow State?

So what is the key to entering this enchanted state? Do you need to practice a certain meditation or learn a spell to get there?

In no way. A flow state is not difficult to achieve and entering one is neither difficult nor strange. You may discover your flow by using the advice that follows:

1. Concentrate on what you like doing.
It is essential to emphasize this. When you are doing something you like, going with the flow is simple. Think back to the last time you engaged in an activity that you enjoyed; I guarantee you scarcely noticed the time passing.

2. Tough but not impossible.

Your assignment should be difficult enough to maintain your focus without becoming overpowering. Simple tasks may be finished quickly and with little effort. However, challenging work will keep you from reaching a flow state since it requires too much effort.

3. Recognize your periods of most production.

Take notes and figure out when you are working your hardest. Although extremely individual, peak production periods are worthwhile to identify. Working on your primary duties during these periods will increase your likelihood of entering a flow state.

4. Avoid becoming distracted.

Choose a location where you can work quietly. If there are people present, shut the door and put up a "do not disturb" sign. Using software like Freedom, you can block internet temptations like social media and other time-wasters. If you can minimize distractions, you will be more effective at entering a flow state.

5. Create a ritual.

Make up a unique set of procedures that you follow each time you begin concentrated work. Go for a little stroll, sip something nice, or inhale a certain fragrance. Your brain will be alerted when you are regularly doing something to concentrate and get into flow mode.

6. Keep going.

Every new ability needs time to develop. Each of these actions demands perseverance and hard work, and you may not succeed right immediately. Try again. Learn from your mistakes and victories since improvement comes only through practice.

Being able to enter a flow state has many positive effects and rewards. You may feel happy and be more productive at work and in your personal life.

Take Solace in the Flow
Being able to enter a flow state has many positive effects and rewards. When you're in a flow state, both your work and personal life are more joyful. You may feel better, work more efficiently, perform better, and be happier.

Put these ideas and advice to use by practicing flow. You'll soon enter the enchanted condition described by Csikszentmihalyi in his past TED Talk:

There is a concentration that, when it gets extreme, brings about bliss and clarity; you know precisely what you want to accomplish at all times.

One of the personal productivity techniques that may help you complete the task that will have the most effect is the flow state.

Like many other productivity techniques, flow state may assist you in focusing for an extended amount of time on the job that is most important.

Cheers to building a life of success and happiness

Printed in Great Britain
by Amazon

36764250R00066